DEAD

Illustrations and Cover Design
by James Louis O'Toole
www.jameslouis.com

Story by Madeline M. Harvey & Jeoff Harris
Words by Benjamin Roustaing, Jeoff Harris,
and Madeline M. Harvey

Edited by Jodi McPhee & Jeoff Harris
Interior Design by Jodi McPhee

ISBN: 979-8-2183023-9-9

www.somedayimgonnabedead.com

Listen along here!

DEAD

by madelline

illustrated by James Louis O'Toole

LOOKS LIKE
I'M AWAKE...

GOT TEAR STAINS ON
MY PILLOW CASE.

YESTERDAY IS YESTERDAY.

BUT TODAY IS TODAY...

...AND I DON'T
FEEL SO GREAT.

THE BLOOD STARTS DRAINING FROM MY FACE THE MOMENT THAT I START TO THINK ABOUT ALL THE THINGS THAT I'M AVOIDING.

BUT THEN A SIMPLE PHRASE
COMES TO MY BRAIN
AND MAKES IT ALL
FEEL BETTER...

...OH SO MUCH BETTER...

Someday I'm gonna be DEAD

Soooooo
DEAD

Time to get out of my head...
and worry just a little bit less...
Someday I'm gonna be
DEAD

Sooooooo
DEAD
Time for me to get out of bed...

...and face the existential dread.
...what?

Do
do
do
do...

...do
do
do
do...

I feel like nothing I'm
doing is right

I feel like lately I'm
wasting my life

cuz I got no direction
always second guessing

everyday I waste a
little more time

RIP

MAYBE
MY MOMENT HAS
COME AND IT'S GONE AND
EVERYBODY IS MOVING ON.

I CAN'T STOP OBSESSING. I'M LIVING WITH THE TENSION...
...OF WISHING I COULD BE WHAT I'M NOT.

BUT THEN A SIMPLE PHRASE COMES TO MY BRAIN AND MAKES IT ALL FEEL BETTER...

...OH SO MUCH BETTER...

Someday I'm gonna be...
DEAD

Soooooo
DEAD

Time to get out of my head...
and worry just a little bit less...

Someday I'm gonna be...
DEAD

Soooooo...
DEAD

Time for me to get out of bed...

and face the
existential dread.

...do
do
do
do...

Someday I'm gonna be...

Do
do
do
do...
la
la
la
la...
...someday I'm
gonna be...

SOMEDAY I'M GONNA BE DEAD.
SO DEAD.

TIME FOR ME TO GET OUT OF BED
AND FACE THE EXISTENTIAL DREAD.